MAKE IT BREAK IT

Pat Thomson

Illustrated by
Martin Salisbury

OXFORD
UNIVERSITY PRESS

In his dream, he was running, running. Behind him, he could hear her feet. He could hear the fast slap, slap of her trainers. His heart was pounding, he was gasping for breath. The girl was coming nearer, nearer.

In front of him was the river. There was nowhere else to run.

Suddenly, he was awake.

He stared round at his models. He was in his own bedroom but he could still hear that breathing. There was a little whining noise and he turned his head.

"It's you," Ollie sighed and gazed into Jack's big, brown eyes. Jack thumped his tail gently on the floor.

"Time to get up," yelled Mum.
She was always in a hurry.

"Mum, I feel sick.
Can I stay at home?"
said Ollie.

His mother was angry.

"There's nothing wrong with you. Get dressed!"

She didn't understand. He *really* felt sick. It was because of the girl.

After breakfast, Ollie took Jack for his walk. They usually went down the road, round the building site and back through the narrow lane between the older houses.

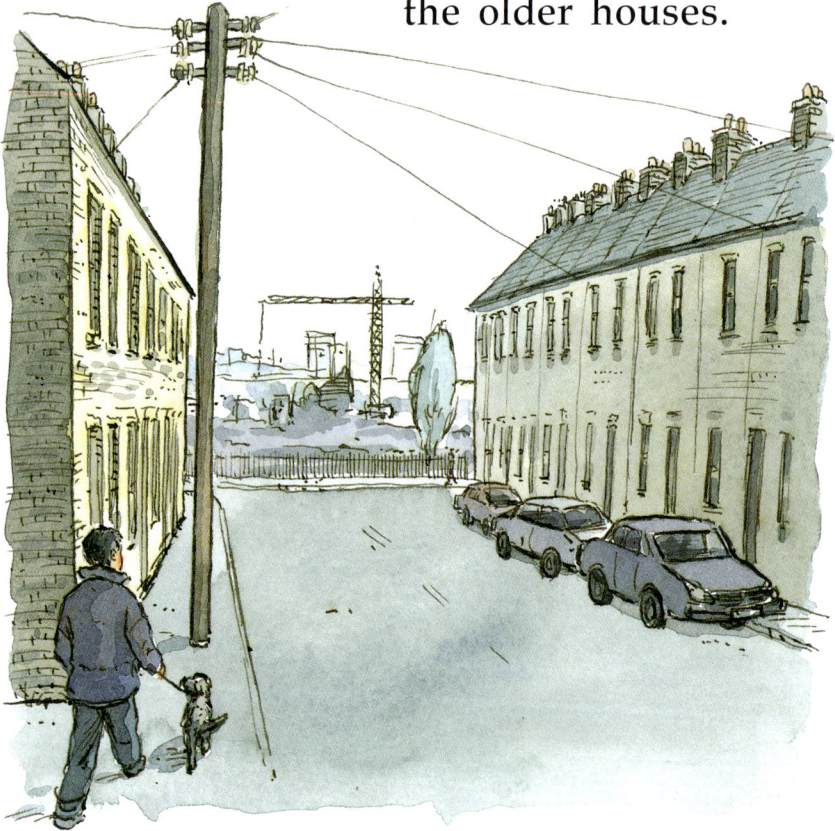

Jack walked, Ollie talked.

"I hate school, Jack. She's always there. She's always picking on me, and the others laugh. I hate her."

Jack whined. He was a good friend. Now they could hear the machines on the building site. They stopped to watch the big digger. Old Mr Crowe was also watching.

"I used to play here," he said. "It will all be gone in a week. Knocked flat."

Ollie nodded.

They watched the big demolition ball.
It swung heavily, then crashed into a wall.
Ollie could still see rooms and staircases.
A house without its skin.

Watching it, feeling a bit afraid, Ollie forgot school for a little.

Time to go back.

Time to go to school.

Time to face the girl.

Ollie walked to school very slowly. He felt sick and his head ached. He waited outside until he saw everyone line up in the playground. Then he slipped through the gates and joined his class.

The girl was right at the front but she was watching.

"It's Ugly Ollie," she shouted.

"What's the matter, Jade?" asked Mrs Roberts, shutting the register. "Why are you holding your nose?"

"It's nothing, Mrs Roberts," said Jade. She flicked back her hair and smiled. The teachers did not know what she was like.

Jade was too clever.

"Well, pay attention. Today, we start our new project," said Mrs Roberts.

"The subject is *The School We Would Like*. What if we could build a new one? What would we like?"

"Somewhere for pets," said Adam.

"Somewhere shady to sit," said Katy.

"A swimming pool," said Jade. "I could wear my new swimsuit."

"And you, Ollie?" asked Mrs Roberts.

Ollie jumped, then sank down in his seat. Mrs Roberts waited.

"I don't know," he said, "but we could build models of our ideas." He knew about models. He built them all the time. He was good at models.

"Yessss!" said Adam. "I'll build my place for pets."

"Excellent!" beamed Mrs Roberts. "We will all make a model of part of the school and write something about it. Then we'll put them together. We'll invite Mr Neal to see them." Mr Neal was the Head. "He might take the hint and make some changes!"

Mrs Roberts always got very excited about projects.

Mrs Roberts wrote all their ideas on the board. Ollie kept quiet. They would only laugh at him.

"Ollie can't think of anything," said Jade, loudly. "He's so thick!"

Katy giggled. But Ollie was drawing. Mrs Roberts noticed.

"That's enough, Jade," she said. "Ollie is planning his model. What is it, Ollie?"

"A tower," said Ollie, "to climb."

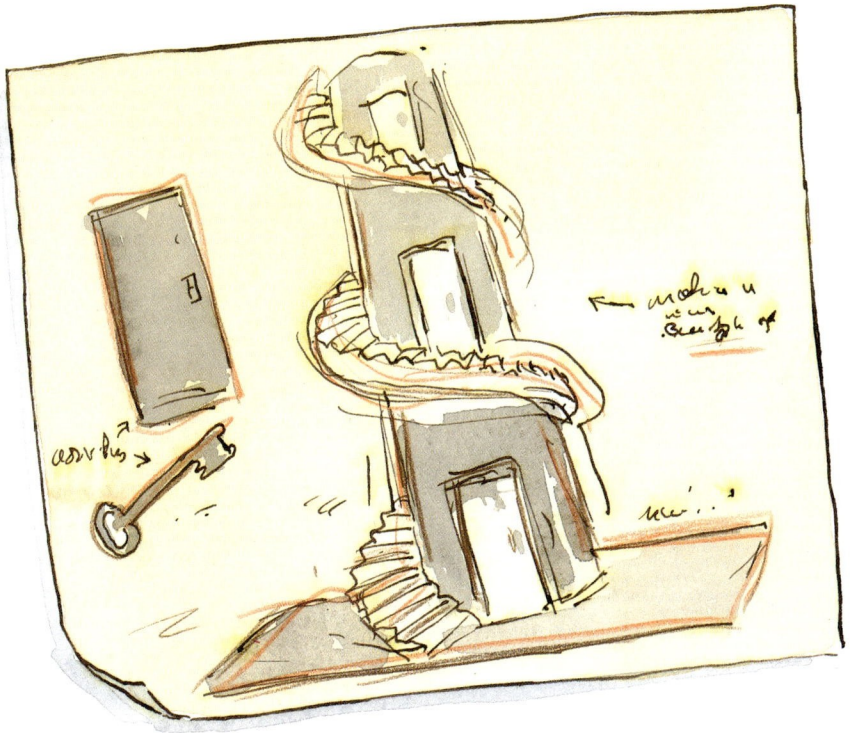

Ollie remembered the building site.
The walls had crashed down but the rooms
and stairs were still there.

He was drawing a mysterious tower. You
could climb higher and higher. Some rooms
would be locked. Only he would have the
key. Only some people would be allowed
to climb.

Jade would be left behind.

He began to build his model. Adam was interested.

"Ollie's tower is really clever," he said. Katy came to look.

"How do you make those tiny stairs?" she said. "And your doors really open!"

Other people came to look, too.

"You're very good at models, Ollie," smiled Mrs Roberts.

Jade was frowning. When Mrs Roberts moved away, she came to look.

"It's rubbish," she said. "Anyway, he smells." She pulled Katy's arm.

"Come and help me. My swimming pool is going to be brilliant."

Katy went, but Adam stayed to talk about making models.

By the middle of the week, everyone agreed that Ollie's tower was the best model.

Jade's was good, too. The swimming pool had an underwater picture of the sea-bed. She had built a good diving-board.

But Ollie was worried. Whenever anyone praised his model, Jade picked on him.

Jade stood up, her face tragic.

"Oh, Mrs Roberts, I'm so sorry."

The class gathered round.

"Poor Ollie," said Mrs Roberts. "It was such a good model." She hadn't seen what happened, but some of the class had.

"Tell Mrs Roberts," whispered Adam.

"It would only make things worse," said Ollie.

At breaktime, Mrs Roberts went for her coffee while the children finished their models.

Adam was angry.

"It's not fair, Jade," he said. "I saw you trip Ollie."

"It was an accident," she smiled.

No one smiled back. They stood round her. The class was no longer on her side.

Jade backed away and sat down. Adam grinned.

"You just sat on your model, Jade!"

Mrs Roberts hurried in as Jade started to howl.

"Oh no!" she wailed, "not another!"

Then Ollie spoke up.

"I can mend both models," he said. "If you can make models, you can mend them."

At the school gates, Mum was waiting with Jack.

"I finished early," she said.

"I had a good day," said Ollie as they walked. "Everyone liked my model. I got a merit."

"Excellent!" said Mum. "Oh look, the demolition is finished. Now they can start to build again."

"A new beginning," smiled Ollie.